THE 7 SPIRITUAL HABITS THAT WILL CHANGE YOUR LIFE FOREVER

ALSO BY ADAM HOUGE

THE 7 SPIRITUAL HABITS

THAT WILL CHANGE YOUR LIFE FOREVER

ADAM HOUGE

CONTENTS

INTRODUCTION

BECOMING A HIGHLY spiritual Christian needs to be the goal of every believer. How we relate to God determines our salvation. Love in itself is an action. The believer, through love, should be fervently seeking the Lord night and day in order to grow nearer to Him.

By pressing hard into Christ, you can have a security in your salvation. Never will you be in question of whether you "will make it or not." But you will always know with the utmost confidence that when you breathe your last, you will be going home.

Those that dedicate their entire lives to the Lord begin to rise above the rest. That is because some people come to Christ with "baggage" they bring along. They halfheartedly accept Christ while not wanting to let go of a couple things. Yet to call Jesus Lord suggests that a person will drop all things to be wholly devoted to Him. If we are not set apart for the purpose of God, then we can become influenced into sin and unrighteousness. As it is written,

> "Do not be deceived: 'Evil company corrupts good habits.'"
>
> 1 Corinthians 15:33

Therefore it is necessary to grow in the good habits while separating ourselves from the bad influences. In this book, we will distill the habits down to the seven most productive ones. If practiced properly, they will bleed over into every other category of life and drive you to become a highly spiritual Christian.

BECOMING THE LOVE OF CHRIST

"By this all will know that you are My disciples, if you have love for one another."
JOHN 13:35

L OVE IS THE fulfillment of the Law. It is the very essence of who and what God is. Even as it is written,

> "And we have known and believed the love that God has for us. God is love, and he who abides in love abides in God, and God in him."
>
> 1 JOHN 4:16

It goes without saying that Christians need to be loving. But sometimes the definition of love gets forgotten by some through the process of time. We get so caught up in providing for our own families that some of us forget to provide for others as well.

There is always someone in need in the church. There is always someone in need of a blessing. We tend to help those around us who are our friends, but without realizing it, we push off the needs of those who aren't—even though they are our family in Christ. But before you ever knew Christ, He sacrificed Himself for you. Before He ever had a relationship with you, He was seeking to deliver you.

If we are to love like He does, then we need to have open eyes for those who need deliverance around us. There are many brethren who need it, and it is always good to start with the household of God. As it is written,

> "Therefore, as we have opportunity, let us do good to all, especially to those who are of the household of faith."
>
> GALATIANS 6:10

But does God really call us to offer our lives for our brethren? Or is this only a special love God has toward us? What do we read?

> "By this we know love, because He laid down His life for us. And we also ought to lay down our lives for the brethren."
>
> 1 JOHN 3:16

So we must be willing to lay down our lives for our brethren. Yet is this calling in the sense of life and death only? Or are we required to share the things of this world to produce equality among us? But as the scriptures go on to say,

> "But whoever has this world's goods, and sees his brother in need, and shuts up his heart from him, how does the love of God abide in him?
>
> My little children, let us not love in word or in tongue, but in deed and in truth."
>
> 1 JOHN 3:17–18

This sense of equality doesn't enter the modern mind. Today we are all so focused on furthering ourselves that we forget to love one another fervently in our times of need. This thinking has largely been given to us by the influence of the cultures around us, such as the "American Dream." Yes, we'll give a meal to a homeless brother but what about a home? If we are to meet his need, then we should give him a place to live.

Yet believers today are frightened by the thought of giving until it hurts. "He's on the streets, and maybe I will be too!"

Seek the Lord on what you should do. Never turn down an opportunity to love a brother in deed and in truth. If you turn down this opportunity, you are not made perfect in love. A spiritual person will seek to live by all the fruits of the Spirit. And what is the first listed fruit of the Spirit? Love.

If then you want to be spiritual, first walk in love. If we abide in love, then we abide in Christ. By abiding in His Spirit, love comes naturally, and we become more of a spiritual creature.

Through perfect love we fulfill the law and thus are justified. Through a pure, loving heart we can see God. As it is written,

> "Blessed are the pure in heart, for they shall see God."
>
> MATTHEW 5:8

And what better way is there to purify the heart than with the love of God? But as we also read,

> "Since you have purified your souls in obeying the truth through the Spirit in sincere love of the brethren, love one another fervently with a pure heart."
>
> 1 PETER 1:22

Seeing that love both justifies us and purifies us, we ought to make it our aim to grow in love always. We must pursue the full meaning of it and grow in equality toward one another. Love doesn't beat around the bush; it hits straight to the heart and fulfills the need. As it is written,

> "If a brother or sister is naked and destitute of daily food, and one of you says to them, 'Depart in peace, be warmed and filled,' but you do not give them the things which are needed for the body, what does it profit?"
>
> JAMES 2:15–16

If someone needs a home, then give them one. If they need food, then feed them. Jesus tells you to give food and drink to your enemy and show them love. If then He commands us to meet the needs of our enemies, how much more so should we meet the needs of our brethren?

Are we not a family in Christ? And what do loving families do? They have equality with one another. Even when they are old, if a sibling is in need, they help each other. This is what a loving family does, and we are commanded to be perfect in God's love. But do the Scriptures actually call us to equality? Yes. As we read,

> "For I do not mean that others should be eased and you burdened; but by an equality, that now at this time your abundance may supply their lack, that their abundance also may supply your lack—that there may be equality.
>
> As it is written, 'He who gathered much had nothing left over, and he who gathered little had no lack.'"
>
> 2 CORINTHIANS 8:13–15

If we allow God to lead us in our works, there should be no reason for fear. If we can't afford to help one another, then maybe we should bring others to the table who can. Many times people fear losing and would rather watch someone else suffer than risk the possibility of suffering themselves.

This is not living out the love of God. But if we are to love our neighbor as ourselves, then we ought to lift a needy brother out of a pit of suffering. We should not fear the harm that *might* come on us but take care of the person that is currently being harmed. Jesus loved us and sacrificed himself to deliver us *knowing* the harm He would receive. Nevertheless, this did not stop Him; He still chose to love us.

We should do likewise as God leads us and convicts us, knowing that we have a Savior who tests our hearts. If then He is testing us, then He has determined a way of delivering us by obedience. Only let yourself be found faithful by the Lord, and love your brethren perfectly.

If we choose to not love due to fear for what could happen, we know that the Scriptures tell us,

> "There is no fear in love; but perfect love casts out fear, because fear involves torment. But he who fears has not been made perfect in love."
>
> 1 John 4:18

Beloved, lay aside your fears; the Lord will take care of you. If we all give and care for one another, then even if you should fall into need, there will be another to lift you out. But if we want to do the right thing, then we need to be the ones to take the first step, even if no one else is. There is no fear in love; there is faith: faith that God loves you and rewards the faithful; faith that God is well pleased with a cheerful giver. It is not what we do religiously that justifies us, but it is both faith and love working hand and hand that justify us. As it is written,

> "For in Christ Jesus neither circumcision nor uncircumcision avails anything, but faith working through love."
>
> GALATIANS 5:6

Circumcision is a work of the flesh and the law. We are not justified by what we do in ourselves nor our striving to be perfect in law but by faith working in love toward others.

Besides, God loves a cheerful giver! As it is written,

> "So let each one give as he purposes in his heart, not grudgingly or of necessity; for God loves a cheerful giver.
>
> And God is able to make all grace abound toward you, that you, always having all sufficiency in all things, may have an abundance for every good work."
>
> 2 CORINTHIANS 9:7–8

Learn to be a cheerful giver and to sincerely care. God is well pleased in such things. Therefore, be a light to those around you through loving-kindness. If you sow in love, you will reap God's grace and loving providence. It is not that we should give expecting to receive. This is not having a perfect heart. Rather, out of pure love, we should give without expecting, knowing that God intends to deliver us and provide for our needs. As it was written in the previous verse,

> "But this I say: He who sows sparingly will also reap sparingly, and he who sows bountifully will also reap bountifully."
>
> 2 Corinthians 9:6

And as it is also written,

> "Blessed is he who considers the poor; The LORD will deliver him in time of trouble.
>
> The LORD will preserve him and keep him alive, And he will be blessed on the earth; You will not deliver him to the will of his enemies.
>
> The LORD will strengthen him on his bed of illness; You will sustain him on his sickbed."
>
> Psalm 41:1–3

Therefore walk in love, and God will be your salvation in everything. Love is the very center of a spiritual person because God is the essence of love. Become the love of God toward others, and learn to die to yourself. Love is the beginning of life, and life is the beginning of a relationship with God.

DILIGENT STUDY OF THE SCRIPTURES

*"Be diligent to present yourself approved
to God, a worker who does not need to be
ashamed, rightly dividing the word of truth."*
2 TIMOTHY 2:15

A HIGHLY SPIRITUAL BELIEVER understands their foundation. They seek to be firmly planted in truth and pure doctrine. Knowing scripture and rightly applying it are two different things. It is the same as the difference between knowledge and wisdom. Knowledge is stored information, and wisdom is the ability to accurately apply it. But in order to become wise, first you need knowledge.

Sometimes in a Christian walk, other things in life begin to distract us from needful study. Righteousness is obedience to the word of God. So then, if you are seeking to grow in your walk, you must grow in knowledge.

If you have been distracted by day-to-day activities and haven't been digging into the Scriptures, then you need to make it a habit to read daily. Set aside some time to read and grow. Make it your habit to grow daily.

If you are always seeking to grow, you will grow. It goes without saying, but sometimes with a busy life, we tend to forget these rudimentary things. Therefore we should make it our aim and pressing effort to grow in the Lord daily. If God is infinite, then everything there is to know about Him must be infinite as well. Seeing that we are not infinite, if we want to know the Lord more, then we should always be growing.

The day a wise man has said in his heart, "I am wise," is the day he has assuredly become a fool for he has ceased from pursuing wisdom. But the man that says, "I am not wise enough," is an all-consuming fire. Though you give him wisdom, much like giving fuel to a fire, he will never be satisfied nor will he say, "Enough."

Beloved, pursue wisdom, and grow in the word. An infant grows quickly when it drinks the milk deeply. Therefore,

> "as newborn babes, desire the pure milk of the word, that you may grow thereby."
>
> 1 Peter 2:2

We are consuming creatures. We eat until we die. There are thousands of pounds of food an individual goes through before they die. If then you are what you eat, let your mind eat of wisdom. Do not stop devouring it even as you will not stop devouring food.

Let the wisdom found in the mind of Christ be your sustenance, and let His Spirit be your water. Eat and drink deep of God and so find strength for your weary soul.

Do not cease to read the word nor cease growing in it. The more you read, the more you'll know. And the more you know, the closer you will get to the Lord in a relationship with Him. Why? Because you are diligently seeking to practice the things you read as a faithful Christian.

Now, as you read the word, certain things will pop out at you from the pages. These are things that God wants you to be learning and meditating on. Take the time to study those things that you may fully understand them. Do not just assume the meaning of the scripture, but always be objective in your studies. You may find out that the scriptures may be saying something different from what you believed for years.

Therefore make knowledge of the truth your priority. Just because you think something is the truth doesn't mean it is truth. Rather, let God tell you the meaning behind the scriptures. He will interpret them to you through the Holy Spirit. As we read,

"These things we also speak, not in words which man's wisdom teaches but which the Holy Spirit teaches, comparing spiritual things with spiritual."

1 CORINTHIANS 2:13

Seeing that God will speak the Scriptures to you, it is good to learn to be quiet within yourself. Learn to listen inwardly to the Holy Spirit in a daily walk. Listen carefully as you read the word. If there is anything that is speaking to you, it's not that the Scriptures are speaking to you but it's the Holy Spirit. Listen to the Holy Spirit, and whatever speaks out to you, meditate on that. Grow in it and memorize it.

If you struggle with memorizing the scriptures, I wrote another book on that topic called *How to Memorize the Entire Bible in No Time Flat*. It does not contain the same old tips and tricks most use for memorization; rather, it discusses how the Holy Spirit can help you retain any and every scripture He speaks to you.

Basically, if you hear something speaking to you, start there for memorizing. Do not try to memorize the "good verses" or the "typical ones" that everybody else suggests. Memorize what God is speaking to you now and today. Those are the lessons He wants you to learn. So be a good student and memorize them, just like we did with topics at school.

At school, we memorized what the teacher gave us, not what we thought was good, or we wouldn't get the grade. Likewise, God, being our teacher, knows what is best, and He will guide you through the Scriptures according to your individual needs for growth. Follow along with Him, and before you know it, you will have memorized a large portion of the entire Bible.

He is always teaching us lessons in our walk. What He teaches us needs to be our main priority. Not what the pastor teaches, but what God teaches through him. For it is the pastor who is used by God to plant and water, but it is God who teaches us and grows us. As it is written,

> "So then neither he who plants is anything, nor he who waters, but God who gives the increase."
>
> 1 CORINTHIANS 3:7

God will be the One who increases us in wisdom as He teaches us lessons for growth through life. Seeing that it is His will for you retain the current lesson, He will assist you with retaining wisdom if you lean on Him in faith.

As it is written,

> "If any of you lacks wisdom, let him ask of God, who gives to all liberally and without reproach, and it will be given to him.
>
> But let him ask in faith, with no doubting, for he who doubts is like a wave of the sea driven and tossed by the wind.
>
> For let not that man suppose that he will receive

anything from the Lord; he is a double-minded man, unstable in all his ways."

James 1:5–8

God wants us to know the entire word, but He likes it when His students pay attention. If we blow off His lesson and try to meditate on something irrelevant to the teaching He is giving us, we are not having upright hearts. Yes, the lessons of the word of God all work hand in hand, but God guides us through the textbook.

When we read textbooks in school, we follow along with the teacher rather than jumping ahead. Likewise, we must follow along with the Lord as He teaches us from the word. Yet some have a habit of trying to memorize everything, whether it pertains to their immediate situation in life or not. But if you follow along with God and memorize what He gives you to memorize, then He will be your strength to retain it. In the end, you will be able to memorize a great amount by the power of His Spirit through faith.

And doesn't faith come by *hearing* His word? Whatever the Holy Spirit speaks to you is what you need to be growing in. Even as it is written,

"So then faith comes by hearing, and hearing by the word of God."

Romans 10:17

If then faith comes by hearing, then listen to the Holy Spirit. We couldn't even come to Christ unless we heard God tugging at our hearts. As it is also written,

> "No one can come to Me unless the Father who sent Me draws him; and I will raise him up at the last day."
>
> JOHN 6:44

But that we should be listening to the Holy Spirit and be taught by Him is evident. For it goes on to say,

> "It is written in the prophets, 'And they shall all be taught by God.' Therefore everyone who has heard and learned from the Father comes to Me."
>
> JOHN 6:45

Beloved, come to the Lord and sit at His feet as you read. Learn to listen to *His* teachings as He interprets the word for you. He will give you what you need, for He knows all that you need.

If you are having a hard time remembering and applying the scriptures, He will not leave you without help. Beloved, do you not remember? The Holy Spirit is your Helper sent from God! He shall strengthen you and give you what you need to retain the word and apply it daily. Only have faith, and all things will be possible for you through Christ Jesus. Believe that God will help you, and say in your heart,

> "I can do all things through Christ who strengthens me."
>
> PHILIPPIANS 4:13

Believe it! God will do it! I have seen in my own personal walk God helping me retain scripture. I had a difficult time memorizing, but when I learned to lean on Him in faith, suddenly I started memorizing entire books in single sittings. It would usually take a day, but I was able to memorize an entire book or epistle word for word in a day. This is not my own strength but the power of God at work in me. He also will work in you by this power.

> "But from those who seemed to be something— whatever they were, it makes no difference to me; God shows personal favoritism to no man..."
>
> GALATIANS 2:6

God will do likewise with you because He favors no one. He will bless you according to your faith, even as Jesus said to the blind men in Matthew 9:29: "According to your faith let it be to you."

Yet this concept of seeking God for wisdom is not new. It goes back to the beginning of time and has much to do with the Fall of man. During the first sin, Eve was tempted by the fruit from the tree of knowledge of good and evil. She desired the wisdom it gave. As it is written,

> "So when the woman saw that the tree was good for
> food, that it was pleasant to the eyes, and a tree desir-
> able to make one wise, she took of its fruit and ate."
>
> GENESIS 3:6

Is the pursuit of wisdom wrong? It can be, depending on where we are looking to get that wisdom from. God is the source of all wisdom and made everything that we call knowledge.

Therefore, beloved, seek Him directly for it. He made it after all! Won't He know it best? If you seek Him, He will speak it to you. Eve made the mistake of not seeking God for wisdom but was tempted by the thought of reaching out and taking wisdom for herself. Now think about it: How do you suppose this world would have been different if Eve would have asked God for it rather than taking it of herself? "God, will you grant me wisdom?" Do you think He would tell her no? But what did He say to Solomon?

> "Then God said to Solomon: 'Because this was
> in your heart, and you have not asked riches or
> wealth or honor or the life of your enemies, nor
> have you asked long life—but have asked wisdom
> and knowledge for yourself, that you may judge My
> people over whom I have made you king —wisdom
> and knowledge are granted to you; and I will give
> you riches and wealth and honor, such as none of
> the kings have had who were before you, nor shall
> any after you have the like.'"
>
> 2 CHRONICLES 1:11–12

It's obvious that little can please God more than praying wholeheartedly for wisdom and understanding. It is absolutely in the will of God for Him to give you wisdom, as we outlined in James 1:5–8. Therefore, beloved, seek it by faith. Persist in the word so that you'll become a spiritual creature. God will shower you with heavenly riches that can neither corrode nor fade nor any thief break in and steal—blessing reserved in heaven for you.

Be like Solomon and seek God for wisdom and understanding. Pursue Him in the word, and meditate on what He is speaking to you. He adores a good listener because faith comes by hearing and righteousness comes by practicing faith.

The spiritual person seeks to grow in the word daily. Be a hungry little sponge that can never be satisfied. Absorb the pure milk of the word, and seek God for more. He will grant it to you because wisdom gives life. As it is written,

> "…wisdom gives life to those who have it."
>
> Ecclesiastes 7:12

God loves you and will give you everything you need to have life and grow in Him. As a mother is with her nursing child so God cannot forget you. He will lead you and guide you tenderly. He will nourish you with the pure milk of His word. Therefore, beloved, drink deep of the wisdom of God and grow thereby. If you do this, you shall become fully pleasing to the Lord.

SELF-DISCIPLINE

*"But I discipline my body and bring it into
subjection, lest, when I have preached to
others, I myself should become disqualified."*
1 CORINTHIANS 9:27

SELF-DISCIPLINE NEVER COMES naturally, yet it is one
of the most important aspects of a Christian walk. If
we do not learn to curb the appetite of the flesh, temptation can get out of control. But if we discipline ourselves
to abide daily in the Lord's presence, we will have security in Christ.

Even as Paul has said, "lest when I have preached to
others, I myself should become disqualified." This statement tells us that if we allow the desires of the flesh to
rule over us, we may lose our salvation. You cannot both
walk in sin and be saved at the same time. As we read,

> "For those who live according to the flesh set their minds on the things of the flesh, but those who live according to the Spirit, the things of the Spirit.
>
> For to be carnally minded is death, but to be spiritually minded is life and peace.
>
> Because the carnal mind is enmity against God; for it is not subject to the law of God, nor indeed can be."
>
> ROMANS 8:5–7

People seem to think that once they have God's grace, sin doesn't have an effect anymore. But why did Jesus die in the first place? To extinguish the ember of sin and bring the freedom of life to man by His power.

Receiving Christ as Lord isn't a "get out of jail free" card. If we walk in sin, then our hearts are not sincere toward Him. If our hearts are not sincere, then we do not find His grace. But by repentance, His grace is manifested toward us.

Rather than walking in a pattern of repentance and grace, we should step forward by the power of the Holy Spirit into a walk of victory and praise. God is able to overcome all things in us and through us. Therefore, beloved, be diligent to abide in Him. We are required to tame the flesh and sit daily in His Spirit. And by meditating on His presence, we will find strength to overcome all things.

Your flesh and your spirit are two different creatures. Your spirit is a noble creature in Christ. But your flesh is a brute beast, and its only objective is to devour. It is up to you which creature you will feed.

If you feed the beast of the flesh, it will grow in strength and be able to subdue and overcome the spiritual creation inside of you. There is no balance between the two. There is only a struggle for dominance and survival. If you only feed the flesh, then the spiritual creature will grow thin and weak. It will become difficult for you to resist sin and temptation because your spirit is weak and needs to "eat of the Lord." As Jesus said,

> "'Most assuredly, I say to you, unless you eat the flesh of the Son of Man and drink His blood, you have no life in you.
>
> Whoever eats My flesh and drinks My blood has eternal life, and I will raise him up at the last day. For My flesh is food indeed, and My blood is drink indeed. He who eats My flesh and drinks My blood abides in Me, and I in him.
>
> As the living Father sent Me, and I live because of the Father, so he who feeds on Me will live because of Me."
>
> JOHN 6:53–57

If you feed the spiritual creature with the things of Christ, then it will grow strong and the flesh will wither. Your spirit will be strengthened by God to overcome the flesh, and thus it will make you a more spiritual person. Therefore we are required to be self-disciplined to feed the spirit with Christ.

There will be times that you don't feel like seeking the Lord. Something inside you would rather watch TV, play a game, or pop in a movie. This particularly may happen after a long day of work. We have been taught by the culture around us to relieve the stress of the flesh with play and entertainment. But as Christians, we are called to rest in the Lord to find new strength in Him. As it is written,

> "Come to Me, all you who labor and are heavy laden, and I will give you rest."
>
> MATTHEW 11:28

So if you find yourself feeling like you don't want to seek God, then you have to apply self-discipline. Seek God anyway because you love Him and it's the right thing to do. If you love the Lord, you will seek Him. So discipline yourself to come out from everything around you that distracts you from God. Learn to sit quietly and alone in God's presence. As it is written,

> "And He said to them, 'Come aside by yourselves to a deserted place and rest a while.'"
>
> MARK 6:31

It is good to find a place to sit alone with the Lord without any distractions. That way you can focus your full attention on Him. Do this, and be disciplined to drown out all the noises of the flesh. This is how many prophets of old sought the Lord. Even Jesus would go alone somewhere to pray. It is good to sit quietly and hide yourself away to be with the Lord.

As we read,

> "But you, when you pray, go into your room, and when you have shut your door, pray to your Father who is in the secret place; and your Father who sees in secret will reward you openly."
>
> MATTHEW 6:6

Go to the secret place, and be with the Lord. What do people do when they fall in love? Do they daily announce it from rooftops? Or do they seek a quiet place to be alone and focus on each other? True intimacy comes from the alone time two lovers spend together.

Therefore if you want to be more intimate with the Lord, seek a quiet place to be alone with Him, just the two of you. Then focus on Him alone. Discipline yourself to put away all other distractions and seek the face of God. Sit in His presence and pray. Do whatever He leads you to do during this time.

If He is tugging at your heart to read the word or worship, then do it. Swiftly obey Him, and be disciplined to do it right away. God loves a servant who is swiftly obedient. The more you listen and obey, the more you will hear God's voice in your life.

So it is good to come out *daily* from the distractions around you and find God in the secret place. Seeking

Him in a distraction-free place is the best way to abide in Him. As it is written,

> "He who dwells in the secret place of the Most High Shall abide under the shadow of the Almighty."
>
> Psalm 91:1

God will cover you with His feathers and protect you from the perils of sin. Judgment will pass over you, and the love of God will abound upon you. Even as the psalm goes on to say,

> "A thousand may fall at your side, And ten thousand at your right hand; But it shall not come near you. Only with your eyes shall you look, And see the reward of the wicked."
>
> Psalm 91:7–8

If you want a constant walk of victory and praise, then be disciplined to seek the Lord. This abiding needs to take place daily. But abiding in Him is so much more than a daily devotion. It is an ongoing process throughout the day. Focus your thoughts on Him, and love Him with all your mind. It is easy for our minds to trail off on idle things.

But if we are disciplined to focus our mental energy on His daily abiding presence, then we will find strength to continue in Him. The more we seek Him, the easier it is to continue in His Spirit throughout the day. And why? Because we are taking the time to feed the spiritual creature while we starve the flesh of its desires.

Now, by starving the flesh of its desires, I mean to say seeking the Lord instead. We do not become strengthened by restraint but by focus. This isn't a call to abstain from fleshly things but to focus on the Lord. Then by the nature of it, we won't be focusing on the flesh.

But if we abstain from things of the flesh, then we are focusing on fighting the flesh rather than sitting in the Spirit of God. But if we ignore the flesh and focus on the Lord, the Spirit will strengthen us to overcome daily struggles and obstacles—including sin and bondage.

If we lack self-control, then we will succumb to a lifestyle of sin. Jesus was not crucified for nothing. He was beaten, whipped, cruelly treated, mocked, and scourged— having had a twisted crown of thorns beat into His scalp. Then they gave him a robe and let the wounds scab into the fabric. Afterward they took the garment by the fringes and tore it off Him to reopen the wounds. In the end, they took all dignity from Him and stripped Him naked then murdered Him on a cross.

Jesus did not go through all of this so that we could come to know Him as Savior then go back to walking in sin. Having Jesus Christ is not a license to sin but an opportunity for freedom and hope. Therefore, beloved, walk in repentance and be self-disciplined to continue in Him.

If you do not want to do the things of Christ, do them anyway. Let your love compel you, and remain disciplined in your conduct. Discipline yourself to love. Love is not a feeling but an action. Some people forget that it is not only a noun, but it can be a verb. Jesus said to Peter, "Do you love me?" This is a verb. In this statement, Jesus is requiring the action of love from us.

If we walk by complacency, then we do not love the Lord. If you don't feel like seeking God but instead obey your fleshly desire, then you do not love the Lord. But if you ignore your desire and seek God anyway even when you don't want to, then you are loving the Lord. Love is a self-disciplined action. Continue in it, seek the Lord, and be self-disciplined in all things.

A LIFE OF WORSHIP

*"I beseech you therefore, brethren, by the
mercies of God, that you present your
bodies a living sacrifice, holy, acceptable
to God, which is your reasonable service."*
ROMANS 12:1

SHOWING GRATITUDE IS a core essential of the Christian faith. Learning to praise God at all times and in all things can be a difficult task. But grace is something we respond to and not only receive. By choosing to worship, we are acknowledging the Lord's sovereignty and love. This can only be approached with a heart of gratitude.

A spiritual person continuously lifts up praises for the goodness of the Lord, even when they cannot see it. God established the need for blind faith when He spoke to Thomas:

> "Jesus said to him, 'Thomas, because you have seen Me, you have believed. Blessed are those who have not seen and yet have believed.'"
>
> John 20:29

The question is, can you believe God is good even when things are hard? Everyone can worship and praise Him during good times. And everyone can have gratitude for the good God gives us. But by blind faith, can you have gratitude for the hardships of life?

Can you still believe God is good and worthy of praise, even when you don't see it? The heart you need to have in these circumstances is a heart of unconditional love.

If you do not praise God in the bad times, then you are not loving the Lord or having faith in Him. If you do not thank Him for the bad times but question Him, you are not made perfect in love. We are commanded to have unconditional love. Yet sometimes we forget that our love for God must be unconditional as well. If you only worship Him when you feel like it or if you only praise Him when things are good, then your love for Him is conditional. If that is the case, beloved, you must repent.

We must always have a mindset of loving God no matter what, much like the marriage vows: "In sickness and health, for richer or poorer, for better or for worse, until death brings us closer to the Lord."

God is always good, and He never changes. Just because the circumstances in our life change doesn't mean He changes. When the winds of life don't blow favorably and when the waves come crashing over, we must keep our eyes fixed on Him in praise. For He is worthy, and His love endures forever.

Now, it can be difficult to do this during extremely difficult trials. But this is the mindset we still need to have going into them. We need to continue to believe that God is good no matter what and that His love endures forever. God gives us all things for the purpose of a greater good.

It's not that He allows some random circumstances to befall us. But with careful consideration, He has given us the trials of our life to stretch us in our faith. But why is this so important? Why do we need to go through so much hardship just to have a little more faith?

It is written,

> "For by grace you have been saved through faith,
> and that not of yourselves; it is the gift of God."
>
> EPHESIANS 2:8

Faith saves us. God increases our faith to increase our eternal security. It is His deepest desire to give you life and life abundantly in Christ. But sometimes we need to go through a difficult valley before we can stand on the mountain of God.

Knowing these points, it is good to remember them and praise the Lord during all circumstances of life. We are even called to give God thanks for the hardships themselves. As it is written,

"In everything give thanks; for this is the will of God in Christ Jesus for you."

1 Thessalonians 5:18

If we are to give thanks in everything, that means *everything*, including the things of adversity.

As it also written,

"'Shall we indeed accept good from God, and shall we not accept adversity?' In all this Job did not sin with his lips."

Job 2:10

But why should we give Him thanks and worship Him for the bad in life? Because we are expressing faith that God intends good through it and not evil. We are also expressing faith that God loves us and gives us all things out of love. Therefore we ought to worship the Lord in the good times and in the times of adversity.

Unending Love Song

A spiritual person makes it a habit to worship all the time, in every situation. All day such a person lifts up an unending love song to the Lord. Keeping in the Spirit is the ultimate goal of this.

What we mean to say is that there are two kinds of abiding. There is the abiding of the Spirit when we first get saved. He never leaves us or forsakes us. But then there is our abiding in Him. He abides in us always, but we are called to "abide back" so to speak.

This is where many people feel the "second outpouring." They feel the rush of God come upon them in salvation, but they continue to feel the rush of God as they worship. This is what it means to sit and abide in His presence.

God is calling us to be sitting in His presence at all times, and worship is one of those many tools to do that. When you worship, do you feel the presence of God surround you? Stay in the light, and don't walk away. Keep in His presence, and sit there with Him. Whenever you feel God when you're doing something, that's what He wants you to be doing. So keep worshipping, and worship all day long inwardly.

Let a never ending love song pour from your heart. When you are getting idle minded and have nothing practical to devote your thoughts to, then worship the Lord. He is worthy of it, so give it to Him!

Show Him your constant gratitude for His goodness in your life. Show Him gratitude even when you can't see it. Thank Him always for everything, and keep the faith always. Be a spiritual creature devoted to a life of song and praise. As it is written,

> "speaking to one another in psalms and hymns
> and spiritual songs, singing and making melody
> in your heart to the Lord,

> giving thanks always for all things to God the
> Father in the name of our Lord Jesus Christ."
>
> EPHESIANS 5:19–20

Have a heart devoted to praise. He deserves it. He gave His life for you and counted all things as nothing compared to having you. Do you not know how much the Lord has loved you? Haven't you seen and heard?

But what is written?

> "Looking unto Jesus, the author and finisher of
> our faith, who for the joy that was set before Him
> endured the cross, despising the shame, and has
> sat down at the right hand of the throne of God."
>
> HEBREWS 12:2

And what is the joy that was set before Him? Some people would suggest it was to sit at the right hand of the Father. But Jesus was there to begin with! He was originally at the right hand of God, being God, and came down as a man to give you hope. Jesus chose to suffer a horrible, brutal death to show you how much He loved you! So what then was His joy? *You are His joy!* And a fulfilling relationship with you was the joy set before Him. Yes He had joy in ascension, by why did He even come in the first place?

To save you from yourself and give you a future and a hope with Him forever. He came down to love you, to set you free, and to bring justice to this world. As it is written,

"I looked, but there was no one to help, And I wondered That there was no one to uphold; Therefore My own arm brought salvation for Me; And My own fury, it sustained Me."

ISAIAH 63:5

God brought salvation to His people through Jesus Christ. Christ is His strong arm. And in justice, the fury of God is upon His adversaries. For this reason He came, for this reason He died: that He could love you and nourish you tenderly in a relationship with Him and that He may bring justice on those who walk contrary to Christ.

Therefore remember His love for you. You are His joy, and He seeks to continuously abide in you. Likewise, seek to continuously abide in Him by worship and praise with a heart of gratitude.

FOLLOWING GOD AND NOT YOUR OWN HEART

"For as many as are led by the Spirit of God, these are sons of God."
ROMANS 8:14

BEING LED IS one of the most important aspects of a Christian walk. Yet there are still many who struggle with understanding this concept. They feel that living out the word of God as they read it is all that God requires of them. However, the Lord also speaks His word to us through the inward abiding of the Spirit.

The main goal is to discern the still small voice within ourselves and obey it. Is it really God speaking? Or our own heart? If we are accustomed to jumping to conclusions, we will find ourselves in the school of hard knocks. For this reason, I'd rather call it jumping to concussions!

When we think we have heard God and are uncertain but step out in faith anyway, we are setting ourselves up for disaster. If "faith comes by hearing, and hearing by the word of God" (Romans 10:17), then we know that our faith should be in His word only. If we do not know that it is His word or His Spirit speaking to us, we need to test. As we read about Gideon,

> "look, I shall put a fleece of wool on the threshing floor; if there is dew on the fleece only, and it is dry on all the ground, then I shall know that You will save Israel by my hand, as You have said."
>
> JUDGES 6:37

It is not that Gideon was putting the Lord to the test. Rather, he was testing to see if it was the Lord speaking to him in the first place that he might walk by faith in the word of God. Even Jesus came with miracles to testify to the words He had that all men might know that His words are from God.

It is important to know who is speaking. You have three voices that speak to you at all times. Your flesh will voice its desires, Satan will speak as an angel of light to deceive you, and the Lord will speak to you quietly, inwardly.

Once we have learned when it is the Spirit speaking, then it is no longer time to question that voice. Listen to it always, and you'll see the Lord working more powerfully in your life. If we follow our own hearts, then we are not submitting to His design. As we read,

> "For we are His workmanship, created in Christ Jesus for good works, which God prepared beforehand that we should walk in them."
>
> EPHESIANS 2:10

We have been created in Christ for works that God has preplanned. We are required to submit to these and not seek our own desires. In this, God tests us: "Will you love Me perfectly and choose My heart over yours? Or will you follow your own heart?"

Although God permits us free will, we are no longer our own. We have been paid for with a price, and Christ has become our Lord and Master. It would be good to submit to the voice of our Master that we may be well pleasing to Him in all things.

We see His word manifested to us in two ways. There is the written Word in the Scriptures and the active Word through the leading of the Holy Spirit. As we established before, it is good to grow constantly in the Scriptures. If we don't grow in knowledge, we can't grow in wisdom. The Scriptures produce knowledge, but the Holy Spirit produces the wisdom of God. Knowledge is the storage of necessary facts, whereas wisdom is the ability to accurately apply knowledge.

Likewise, the Spirit interprets the Scriptures for us

in a way we can understand. He speaks them to us and brings them to remembrance at all times. He takes what was previously written and makes them practical for the here and now. It is He who gives us our understanding that we may walk uprightly before the Lord. As it is written,

> "These things we also speak, not in words which man's wisdom teaches but which the Holy Spirit teaches, comparing spiritual things with spiritual."
>
> 1 Corinthians 2:13

The Holy Spirit compares spiritual things we have learned or have known to the new lessons we are learning. By this method, He expands our understanding of the Scriptures. Then when we have learned them, He reminds us of the Scriptures when it is time to apply them. As it is written,

> "But the Helper, the Holy Spirit, whom the Father will send in My name, He will teach you all things, and bring to your remembrance all things that I said to you."
>
> John 14:26

If you are not sitting quietly in His presence to hear from Him, then you will not hear the things He is bringing to remembrance. It is good for us to sit quietly in our hearts before the Lord to hear from Him like Mary did at the feet of Jesus.

Continue to seek the Lord's will for you. Constantly pray for direction, and do nothing until He answers. It is easy to get caught up in the idleness of life and forget to wait for God's answers. "Why do you need to pray?" I have heard some people ask. "If it's a good thing, then just do it!"

But by "just doing" the good thing, we are neglecting God's best thing. If we always knew what was best, then why would we need a counselor called the Holy Spirit? Rather than forging our own way in Christ, we need to let God lead us. It isn't about what we think is best but what He knows is best. When we have practiced His will consistently, then He will conform our hearts to His will that we may desire it.

When we are led by the Spirit, He is able to work more effectively through us. Balaam wouldn't listen to God's rebuke or direction. As a result, the Lord had to use a donkey to set him in the right direction. We shouldn't need donkey experiences for God to lead us. Even worse, we shouldn't become donkeys used for God's purpose. Rather, we should be His submissive children, always willing to obey.

God doesn't need our hard work or sacrifice. It isn't that He doesn't require it; it's that He hates it. Our works are good-for-nothing filth. We need the Spirit to work righteousness in us and through us. If we could work righteousness on our own, then why would we need a Savior in the first place? But there has never been a person who is good nor has there been any human being that can do rightly. As it is written,

> "The LORD looks down from heaven upon the children of men, To see if there are any who understand, who seek God.
>
> They have all turned aside, They have together become corrupt; There is none who does good, No, not one."
>
> PSALM 14:2–3

And again,

> "But we are all like an unclean thing, and all our righteousnesses are like filthy rags; we all fade as a leaf, And our iniquities, like the wind, Have taken us away."
>
> ISAIAH 64:6

Therefore we should be diligent to seek the righteousness that comes from God. We must continue in the Spirit, not having our own righteousness. In all things, we must seek to please the Father through the inner working of the Spirit. Faith comes from hearing *HIS* word. And notice that the Scriptures say "hearing" and not reading. It is talking about the active voice of the Lord spoken within you and through you. Therefore seek the righteousness that comes from obeying the Holy Spirit and not your own heart. As it is written,

> "and be found in Him, not having my own righteousness, which is from the law, but that which is

through faith in Christ, the righteousness which
is from God by faith."

PHILIPPIANS 3:9

Knowing these things, diligently seek to be led by the Spirit. Righteousness is faith in motion, and faith comes from His word. (Or in other words, "Righteousness is obedience to God's words.") By being led, you will see the full working power of God in your life. You will know when to step out in faith and when to sit back and wait.

If you have ever felt like a fool for stepping out and later realizing it wasn't God, then seek discernment. You will never again suffer this if you learn to sit and wait patiently for His word and to discern who it is that's speaking to you. Many times our own hearts speak to us while we yearn for God to speak. Therefore test the "voice" within yourself, and deny the dictates of your own heart. Beloved, live according to Jesus, and once you have discerned it is His voice speaking to you, then step out in faith, and God will do the work through you.

Continue in the Spirit, and continue to be led by Him. If your understanding of being led hasn't been perfected, then continue to pursue the Lord. Pursue His wisdom and understanding. Pray for it, and God will give it to you.

When you are led by the Spirit, He will work through you more. When we are led by the Spirit, we become spiritual persons.

LIFE OF PRAYER

"pray without ceasing."
1 THESSALONIANS 5:17

PRAYING WITHOUT CEASING can be a difficult concept to grasp, especially when you need to have your attention focused elsewhere. But in this scripture, it is literally saying what it means. God calls us to be in a constant connection with Him at all times. Prayer is more than a lifeline; it's an intimate connection between us and the Father.

We need to be attuned to the Lord when we pray. God loves to hear our hearts. He is a loving and compassionate person, who is always listening to you. As it is written,

> "For the eyes of the Lord are on the righteous, and His ears are open to their prayers..."
>
> 1 PETER 3:12

But it is also good to listen to His Spirit while you pray. He will guide you in what you should pray. Then by praying in the Spirit, you will be praying the will of the Father. Thus you will see more answered prayers. As it is written,

> "Likewise the Spirit also helps in our weaknesses. For we do not know what we should pray for as we ought, but the Spirit Himself makes intercession for us with groanings which cannot be uttered."
>
> Romans 8:26

The Spirit intercedes for us as we pray. But if we are attentive to His speech, we will know what to say. Then the rest, which cannot be expressed with human words, He himself will carry to the Father, even as we just read.

And by praying in the Spirit, we know that we will have an answer from God because we pray according to His will. As the scriptures go on to say,

> "Now He who searches the hearts knows what the mind of the Spirit is, because He makes intercession for the saints according to the will of God."
>
> Romans 8:27

Therefore, beloved, it is good to pray in the Spirit without ceasing. If you continue in prayer, you will be abiding. God will strengthen you in your walk, and you will see Him working around you more abundantly.

Why? Because you are praying without ceasing, God is answering you without ceasing.

Yet some people have struggled with the concept of praying constantly. This is mainly due to a lack of self-discipline, which we talked about in an earlier habit. If you are trying to pray, also pay attention to your thoughts. Sometimes as you pray, a particular topic may cause your mind to trail off. Many times the enemy may try to bring events to remembrance and cause you to replay them in your head rather than pray.

Do not let your thoughts or the enemy distract you, but by faithful persistence, continue in prayer. Watch yourself as you pray, and pay attention to the "trail offs." If you catch them sooner, you will continue in prayer longer. Eventually the devil will give up and your flesh will be self-disciplined enough to focus on what you're praying. As a result, it will be easier to persist in prayer.

Even though we are called to pray continuously, the scriptures also say,

> "Do not be rash with your mouth, and let not your heart utter anything hastily before God. For God is in heaven, and you on earth; Therefore let your words be few."
>
> ECCLESIASTES 5:2

If then we are supposed to have few words, how can we pray without ceasing? The answer begins in the previous verse, which says,

"Walk prudently when you go to the house of God; and draw near to hear rather than to give the sacrifice of fools, for they do not know that they do evil."

ECCLESIASTES 5:1

But what are we listening for, and how can we pray continuously if we must be quiet? We are listening for the Holy Spirit, and when He lays what to pray on our hearts, then we pray. Even as we were saying before, these verses further confirm the need to sit quietly and listen to the voice of the Spirit as we pray.

It also confirms that God is always speaking to you. So the question is, are you listening? Therefore the more you sit and listen, the more you will hear the Lord. His voice will become more apparent because you have trained your ears to listen to Him. His will shall seem less murky because you are better able to understand what He is saying to you.

Therefore beloved, pray with a silent heart. Let God speak to you, and pray what He gives you. Prayer is not one way, but it is a conversation. It is a two-way communication, and you need to learn to listen to the Spirit.

In order to be spiritual, we need to be constantly listening to the Holy Spirit and operating through Him. It is His working in us that justifies us, not our working. When praying, do not relay your messages to God but learn to *relate* to God. In a relationship, we share our hearts with each other. Let Him share His heart with you also. Then you will know and better understand His will in life.

Prayer in itself is one of the most powerful weapons we have in this spiritual war. Therefore by dedicating yourself to a life of prayer, you will see the full power of God working in your life. You will be strengthened against your enemy, and by the Spirit, you will overcome.

Yet some of us still struggle in a walk, not being strengthened. And why? Because we haven't pursued the strength of God in prayer. As it is written,

"Yet you do not have because you do not ask."

JAMES 4:2

If you become accustomed to constantly asking, you will begin to constantly receive. Yet what we receive may not always be what we desire. We, having two natures, do not always desire the best or most spiritual thing. God will always give us what is best for us, but if we pray for worldly things, it doesn't mean we will receive them.

But as a perfectly loving Father, God will give you what is best for your growth. Learn to have a heart of gratitude in prayer. If God answers you and didn't give you what you wanted but something else, thank Him for it. He is giving you what is best out of love. And think of it, the Almighty Eternal God, the All-consuming Fire Who dwells in unapproachable light, took the time to care about your needs and answer you. He, in His sovereign and glorious nature, still counts you as something worthwhile. Who are we that *He* would care? Thousands of kings have risen and fallen and have never cared about a soul. But He does, and we should be grateful for everything He does.

Therefore show gratitude, and persist in prayer. God will give you what you need, and as a result, prayer will be a conduit of strength for you as God answers. By prayer you will grow because God is leading your heart and giving you what you need to draw nearer to Him. By prayer your walk will increase, and you will become a greater light to those around you. A life of prayer makes a stronger, more spiritual Christian.

DEVOTED TO SANCTIFICATION

"Therefore "Come out from among them And be separate, says the Lord. Do not touch what is unclean, And I will receive you.""
2 Corinthians 6:17

SANCTIFICATION MORE OR less means "being separated or set apart for the purpose of God." Many Christians understand that they need to be sanctified but aren't fully aware of everything they are called to do.

When the Levites would prepare for a ceremony, they would be required to consecrate themselves unto the Lord first. This consecration was a calling to be sanctified for the sake of serving the Lord. Similar to the priests, all Christians are servants of the Lord and need to be consecrated unto the Lord.

Being consecrated is so much more than being set apart from one's own sin. It's about being wholly devoted to the service of the Lord, much like how God had the priests sanctify utensils for temple service. Even so, we must be vessels of honor that are always set apart for God's purpose.

Sometimes we set ourselves apart in certain categories of life but not in others. When we are at work, sometimes we act like different people than we do at church. We try to please the people around us for our own gain because we fear losing our job or being shunned. This can happen whenever a person encounters the world, whether at work or with unsaved friends and family. When we fear that we are not made perfect in love.

But God calls us to be ambassadors of Christ. We need to be a light at all times by showing good Christian integrity. To have integrity suggests that you will do the right thing even if no one is looking. Bearing this in mind, in order to have integrity in Christ, it would suggest that we will be like Christ at all times—even when no one is around.

In the end it really comes down to taking our walks seriously in the Lord. We can't have complacent hearts and minds. Love is an action that pursues another person. Therefore beloved, pursue the Lord fervently, and glorify Him in all your conduct. As it is written,

> "As obedient children, not conforming yourselves
> to the former lusts, as in your ignorance; but as

He who called you is holy, you also be holy in all your conduct, because it is written, 'Be holy, for I am holy.'

And if you call on the Father, who without partiality judges according to each one's work, conduct yourselves throughout the time of your stay here in fear;

knowing that you were not redeemed with corruptible things, like silver or gold, from your aimless conduct received by tradition from your fathers, but with the precious blood of Christ, as of a lamb without blemish and without spot."

1 PETER 1:14–19

Being surrounded by the world, we tend to follow some of their philosophies. The people around us assimilate us into their beliefs and practices. Seeking financial safety, a home, a family, and nice things has become the core of many Christians' lives. They work hard, try to get promotions, apply for better jobs, go off to college, but never stop to ask God what He wants first. "If it's a good thing, just go do it!" has become the philosophy of some.

But God loves an obedient servant, not a sacrificial one. Stop setting out to live life your own way. Just because you have an idea of what is good, it doesn't mean you know what is best. God always does, so submit to Him.

Beloved, you are not your own; you have been paid for with a price. Therefore submit to your Lord and Master in all things. Rather than seeking a peaceful life in this world, you should be seeking the Lord and

His direction for you *daily*. At all times, He always wants you to be doing something. Therefore learn to wait quietly for His will. Attune your ears to Him, and be ready to obey. Set aside your own desires and your own heart, and live a selfless life toward God.

The Lord calls us to be separated from those around us. As it is written,

> "Do not be unequally yoked together with unbelievers. For what fellowship has righteousness with lawlessness? And what communion has light with darkness? And what accord has Christ with Belial? Or what part has a believer with an unbeliever? And what agreement has the temple of God with idols? For you are the temple of the living God. As God has said: 'I will dwell in them and walk among them. I will be their God, and they shall be My people.'"
>
> 2 CORINTHIANS 6:14–16

Therefore beloved, separate yourself unto the Lord. Show the world around you that you are not one of them. Being like them doesn't draw them to Christ. They do not have the love of God nor can they comprehend it. But by showing them how far they are from God through the love of God, they will desire Him. There is no goodness in the World. But it is the goodness of the Lord that leads them to repentance. Therefore sanctify yourself in Christ, and become the image of His love. In this, you will be justified, and in this, you will lead many others to salvation.

Sometimes it is necessary to put away unsaved friends or family members. They have no interest in the Lord and are only concerned with turning you away from Him. Although they may not blatantly say to you, "drop the God thing or get out of the family," they may still influence you to follow their opinions, which are contrary to the Lord. As it is written,

> "Do not be deceived: 'Evil company corrupts good habits.'"
>
> 1 CORINTHIANS 15:33

The original Greek word for "habits" is ēthos, which literally means morals. Those that do not have Christ are inherently evil. Therefore they will influence you to do and believe things contrary to Christ. Even if it is a small or subtle thing, it is still dangerous. A little evil is still evil, and a little leaven can fill a whole loaf. As it is written,

> "You ran well. Who hindered you from obeying the truth? This persuasion does not come from Him who calls you. A little leaven leavens the whole lump."
>
> GALATIANS 5:7–9

Therefore we should be diligent to purge the old leaven and walk in the grace of God. Not being conformed to this world but, through love, being transformed in Christ.

If we do not remove the negative influences, we will end up corrupted. If we are corrupted, then we will not walk according to grace in truth. Rather, we will walk in sin and justify it, having had a small change of our doctrine. But God does not justify this. He has grace on a repentant heart willing to follow Him.

Therefore, if you walk contrary to God without repentance, He will not have grace on you but will walk contrary to you. As it is written,

> "And after all this, if you do not obey Me, but walk contrary to Me, then I also will walk contrary to you in fury; and I, even I, will chastise you seven times for your sins."
>
> LEVITICUS 26:27–28

And as the Lord previously said,

> "Then, if you walk contrary to Me, and are not willing to obey Me, I will bring on you seven times more plagues, according to your sins."
>
> LEVITICUS 26:21

If God never changes but always remains the same, why do people think that God won't follow through with His word? We are saved by His word, and God cannot lie. Therefore we must put our faith in all of the Scriptures seeing that they are spoken by Him. Yet some people believe "that was the Old Testament and now we live in the New Testament. That no longer applies because we live in a period of grace." But a period of grace is just that—a period of time.

There is a time coming when He will judge righteously

and declare the former justices. Then grace will be over for those who have not sought it. As it is written,

> "And while they went to buy, the bridegroom came, and those who were ready went in with him to the wedding; and the door was shut. Afterward the other virgins came also, saying, 'Lord, Lord, open to us!' But he answered and said, 'Assuredly, I say to you, I do not know you.'"
>
> MATTHEW 25:10–12

Therefore we should be diligent to keep our lamps burning in full strength. Let us be sanctified to God and His truth. We must pursue His truth with our whole hearts. God will reveal it in the Day of Judgment, and if we were deceiving ourselves or complacent to the truth, His light will reveal it. He does not have grace on those who followed lies, because there is no excuse. And why? Because He has given us every resource that we need through His Holy Spirit to find perfect and complete truth. Why then do some struggle to find it? Because they are not pursuing the Holy Spirit for it. Yet as it is written,

> "However, when He, the Spirit of truth, has come, He will guide you into all truth..."
>
> JOHN 16:13

If then, beloved, His Spirit guides us into all truth, we should be diligent to seek Him for it. Then by faith, He will lead us to it. It can be found; all we have to do is have the heart to search. But there are many truths that have already been laid out for us and cannot be upheaved.

The Old Testament is still practical, alive, and real for today. It was never overwritten by a new set of rules. Yet as Jesus said,

> "Do not think that I came to destroy the Law or the Prophets. I did not come to destroy but to fulfill. For assuredly, I say to you, till heaven and earth pass away, one jot or one tittle will by no means pass from the law till all is fulfilled."
>
> MATTHEW 5:17–18

Therefore, beloved, the curses of the Levitical law are still in effect. The promises of redemption are written there. If then the curses are overwritten, then so are the redemptive promises—unless you honestly think you can pick and choose what you want to believe.

Seeing that these things are true, have fear and come out from the world around you. But in all things obey God. Seek to be led by Him in your relationship and to do all things through Christ. Let the Holy Spirit work through you at all times and so bring glory to the Lord.

Do not approach your worldly acquaintances unless you are led by God to do so. Wait for the Holy Spirit, and if He tugs at you to speak to them and share Christ with them, then do so. But if your relationships with them are not producing the fruit of salvation in them, then pray about what the Lord would have you do. Wait for His answer, and do what He says in faith. He will not keep silent, but the Spirit will speak to you. But be faithful to obey in all things.

Do not relate to the world but share Christ with them that they may relate to God. Rather than trying to create worldly friends, create brothers and sisters in Christ. Your friendships and kinships shall never be lost then.

Separate yourself from all worldly influences. If a person surrounds themselves with bad things, they will become sinful. You will always reap what you sow. Therefore, consecrate yourself unto the Lord, and sow the things of the Spirit in yourself. Seek Him daily, pray, worship, read His word, and always be growing. A plant that doesn't grow doesn't bear fruit. But a plant that always grows is always increasing the amount of fruit it bears.

Being sanctified not only means to separate yourself from sin but it also means to separate from everything that causes sin. Every idol starts as a distraction. If anything distracts you from Christ, you should remove it from your life. If you're going to obey the Lord and be sanctified, then you need to do away with distractions and submit to the Holy Spirit. His leading in life is all that matters. God will give you all the instructions you need for life. All you need to do then is to grow in listening, understanding, and obedience.

But if there is anything in our lives that is not of Christ, then it is worthless. As it is written,

> "Yet indeed I also count all things loss for the excellence of the knowledge of Christ Jesus my Lord, for whom I have suffered the loss of all things, and count them as rubbish, that I may gain Christ."
>
> PHILIPPIANS 3:8

If it isn't Jesus, then count it as rubbish, and conform yourself to Christ. Submit to the will of God as He leads you daily. Come out from the world around you, and be a person of Christ. You have your own culture and your own nation. Do not let them influence you to adapt to their culture, but follow God's method of witnessing that they may adapt to our culture by receiving Christ as Savior.

But that God does not want you relating to the world around you is evident. As it is written,

> "And do not be conformed to this world, but be transformed by the renewing of your mind, that you may prove what is that good and acceptable and perfect will of God."
>
> ROMANS 12:2

And again,

> "Adulterers and adulteresses! Do you not know that friendship with the world is enmity with God? Whoever therefore wants to be a friend of the world makes himself an enemy of God."
>
> JAMES 4:4

And why does He call us adulterers? Because if we submit to anything that is not of Him, we are cheating on Him. Either He is our God or something else is. If we do not follow His doctrine with a sincere heart, then something else is our god.

Now, separating yourself from worldly influences does not suggest only people but anything that distracts you from Christ. Christian literally means follower of Christ. Therefore you need to wholly devote yourself to God, being set apart for His purpose.

Fill yourself and surround yourself with the things of Christ. Rather than watching TV for hours on end, you could be reading the word or praying. This would make you more spiritual by the nature of it. The more you do it, the more your heart will grow for the Lord. As your heart grows for Him, your desire for Him will grow also.

As a result, you will desire the "fun" things of the flesh less and the things of Christ more. But it all takes self-discipline and a faithful heart. God is calling you to do it even as the Scriptures tell us. So do not act like the world around you and constantly entertain the flesh but feed the spirit—as we discussed earlier.

Some people are swallowed up with movies or video games. Some are overtaken by a hobby that is irrelevant to Christ. But if all these things will vanish when Christ returns, why then would we submit to a life of indulgence and play? As it is written,

> "Therefore, since all these things will be dissolved, what manner of persons ought you to be in holy conduct and godliness, looking for and hastening the coming of the day of God, because of which the heavens will be dissolved, being on fire, and the elements will melt with fervent heat?"
>
> 2 Peter 3:11–12

Conduct yourselves with fear and godliness. When you came to Christ, you gave your life to Him. Why then are some people falling back into a lifestyle that excludes Him? You cannot have your foot half in the door of the kingdom and half out and expect to be saved. When God slams that door, you'll be injured in His judgment. It's not worth it!

But it has become the custom of some to put pleasure first and seek God last. Yet as it is written,

> "And do not become idolaters as were some of them. As it is written, 'The people sat down to eat and drink, and rose up to play.'"
>
> 1 Corinthians 10:7

Focusing on a life of play and indulgence is idolatry. Sanctify yourself unto the Lord, and devote yourself to Him. Even as it is written,

> "I beseech you therefore, brethren, by the mercies of God, that you present your bodies a living

sacrifice, holy, acceptable to God, which is your
reasonable service."

ROMANS 12:1

It is only reasonable for you to do this. It is not a
hard thing nor is God asking too much of us. Jesus
was a dying sacrifice for us that by His death and res-
urrection, we could become a living sacrifice for Him.
Sanctify yourself, and be consecrated for His purpose.

This is what the most spiritual believers of all time
have done. Just look at the life of Paul! Likewise, devote
yourself to the Lord, and obey Him always. Seek to
abide in His Spirit daily and be disciplined in it. Be
holy in all your conduct, and grow in the one and only
true doctrine. Give yourself over to seeking the truth.
Pursue it with your whole heart and so please the Lord.
As it is written,

"I have no greater joy than to hear that my children walk in truth."

3 JOHN 1:4

Therefore beloved, do these things, and you will
become a very spiritual Christian.